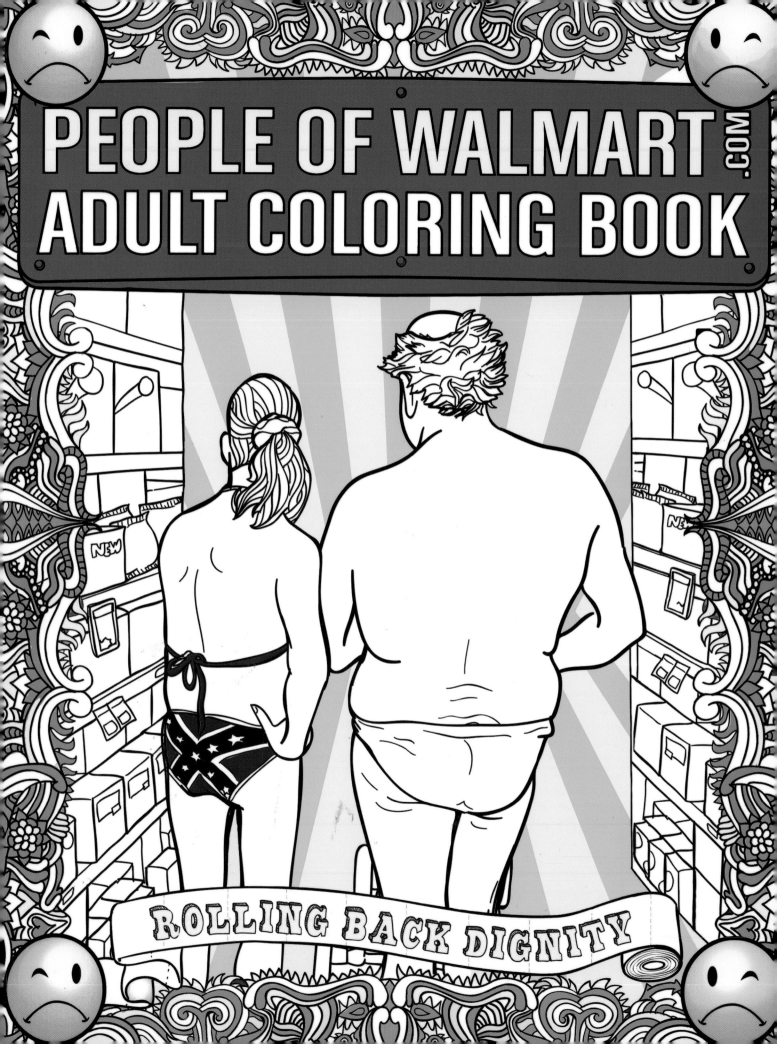

PEOPLE OF WALMART.COM
ADULT COLORING BOOK

DISCLAIMER

We are in no way affiliated or associated with Walmart. We also personally have nothing against Walmart. We, along with most of America, shop at Walmart for nearly everything we need. This book and our website are simply satirical social commentary about the extraordinary sights found at America's favorite store.

Walmart is Americana, baby!

All original artwork is based off of images that have been submitted by the users of www.PeopleofWalmart.com, the rights to which have been granted to ALA Design, LLC.

WARNING:

Some of the images contained in this book are very graphic. We are not responsible if after coloring a page or looking at a picture you have the sudden urge to vomit, stab yourself in the eye, stab a nearby co-worker or friend, jump out of a window, drink bleach, bathe in bleach, clean your eyes with bleach, quit your job and spend the rest of your life in a secluded cave, cut off a limb, become aroused (Really? That's sick!), rally people for a book burning, divorce your partner, skydive without a parachute, join the Taliban, or sell all your assets and give the money to us (actually, that last one is fine). So pretty much, continue reading at your own risk.

ACKNOWLEDGEMENTS:

We'd like to give an enormous thanks to ass-cracks, side-boob, bad parents, jorts, tube tops, cross-dressers, drunks, drugs, muffin-tops, biscuit-bottoms, rednecks, tie-dye, the color-blind, pajamas, pimps, Goths, emos, sluts, states' inability to regulate shit on cars, bad hair, bad tattoos, costume lovers, and every other person out there who loves to express themselves in public. But most importantly, we want to thank our wonderful fantastic amazing magnificent dedicated fans who love to take pictures of the aforementioned people and send them in to us! We honestly could not do any of this without you and we love you all.

ROLLING BACK DIGNITY

ISBN: 978-1-945056-08-6

Published by
Day Drankin' Press

DayDrankinPress.com

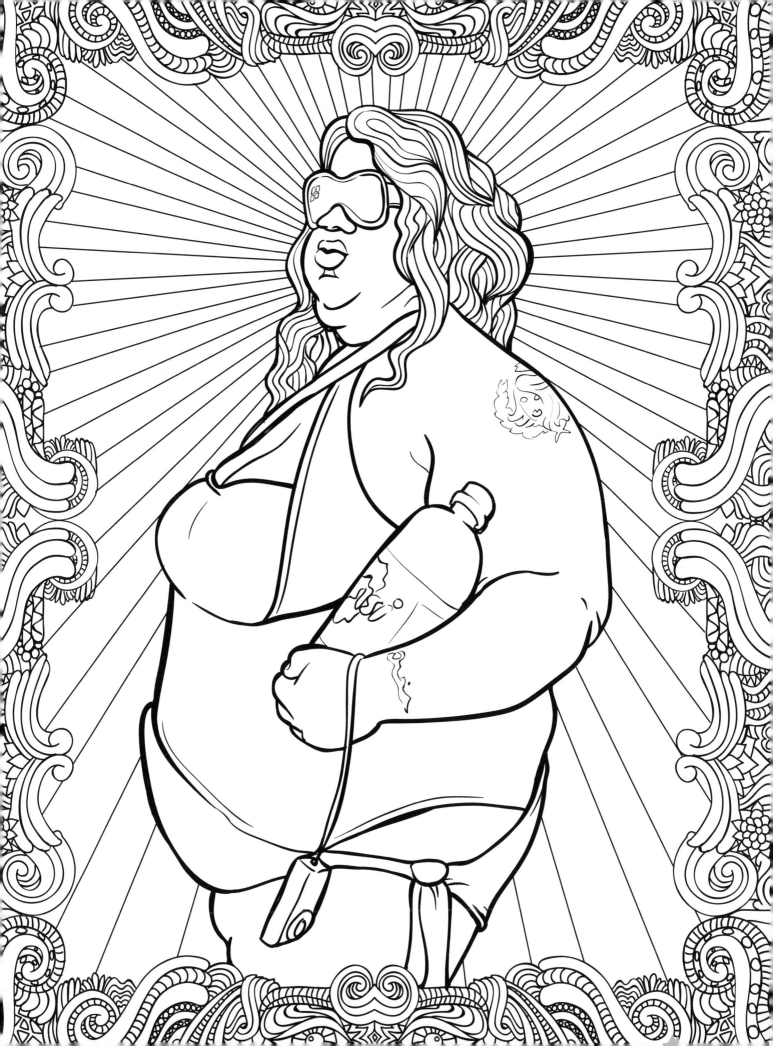

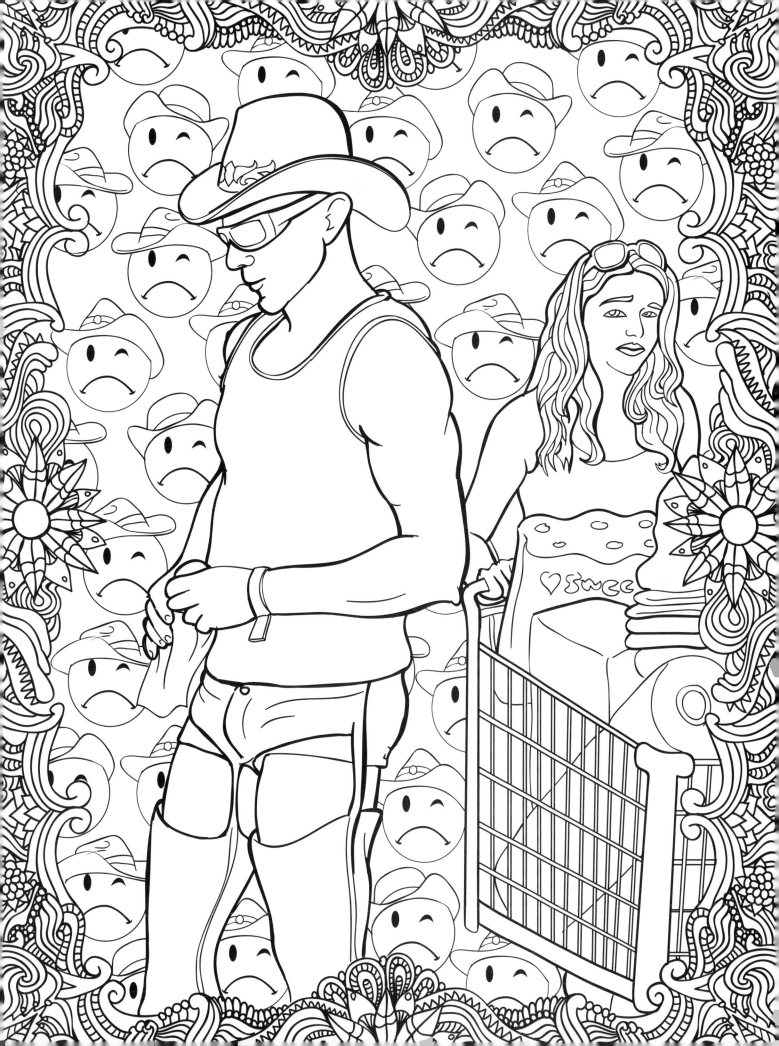

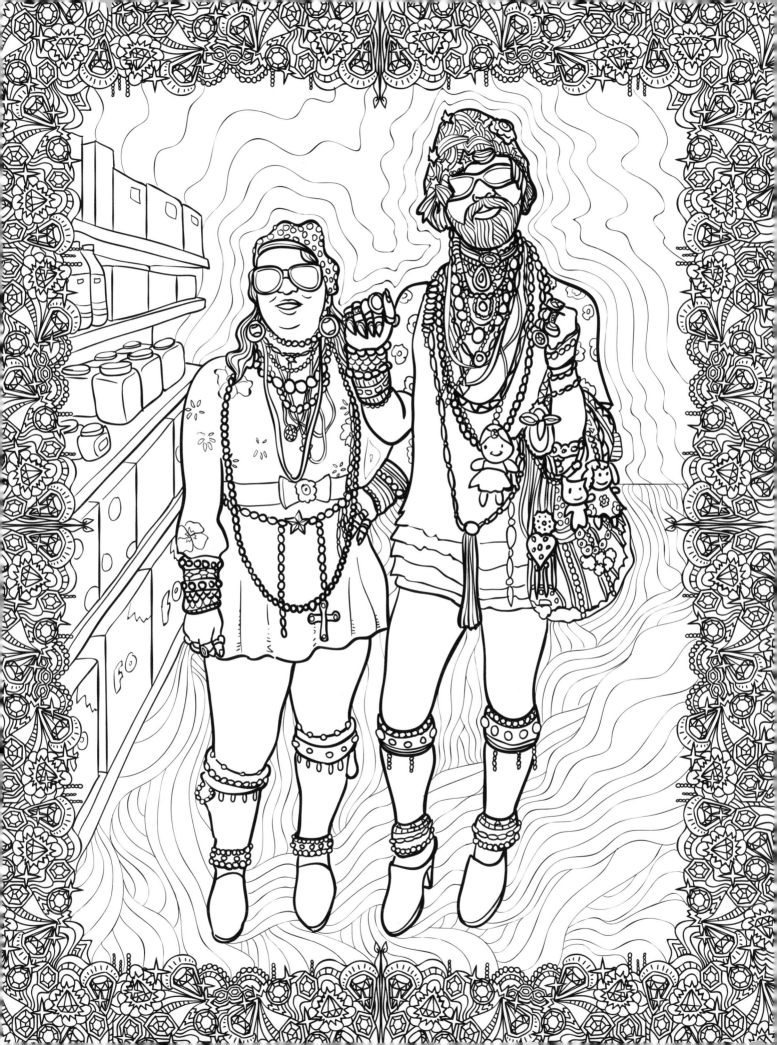

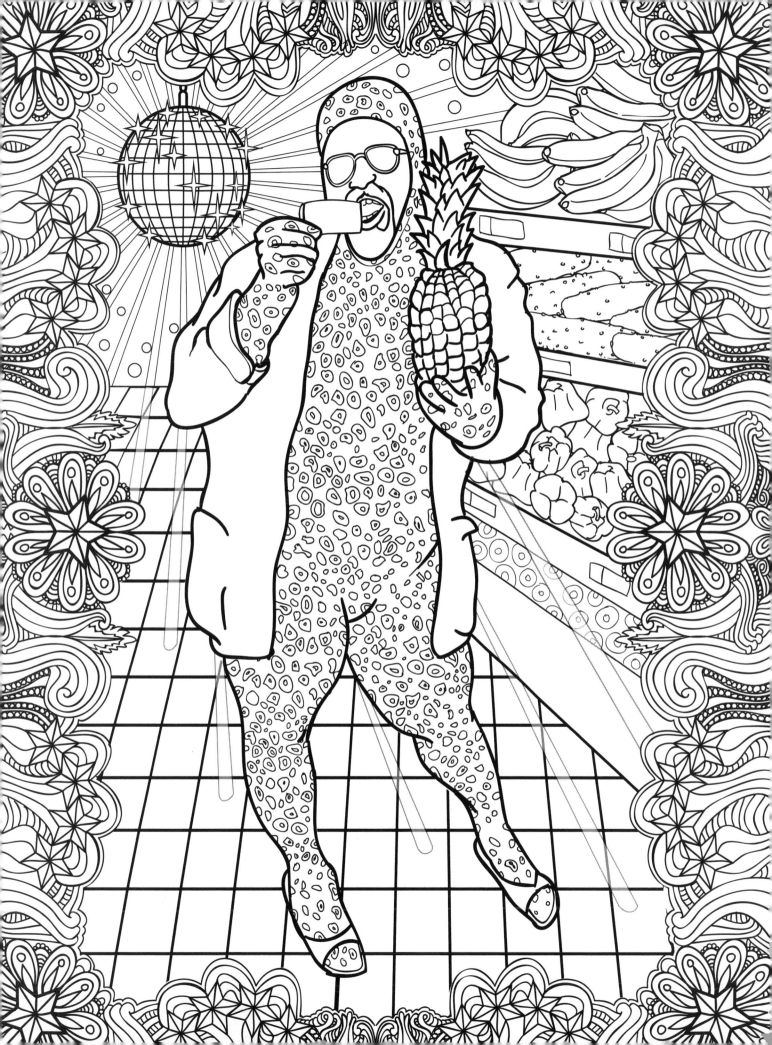

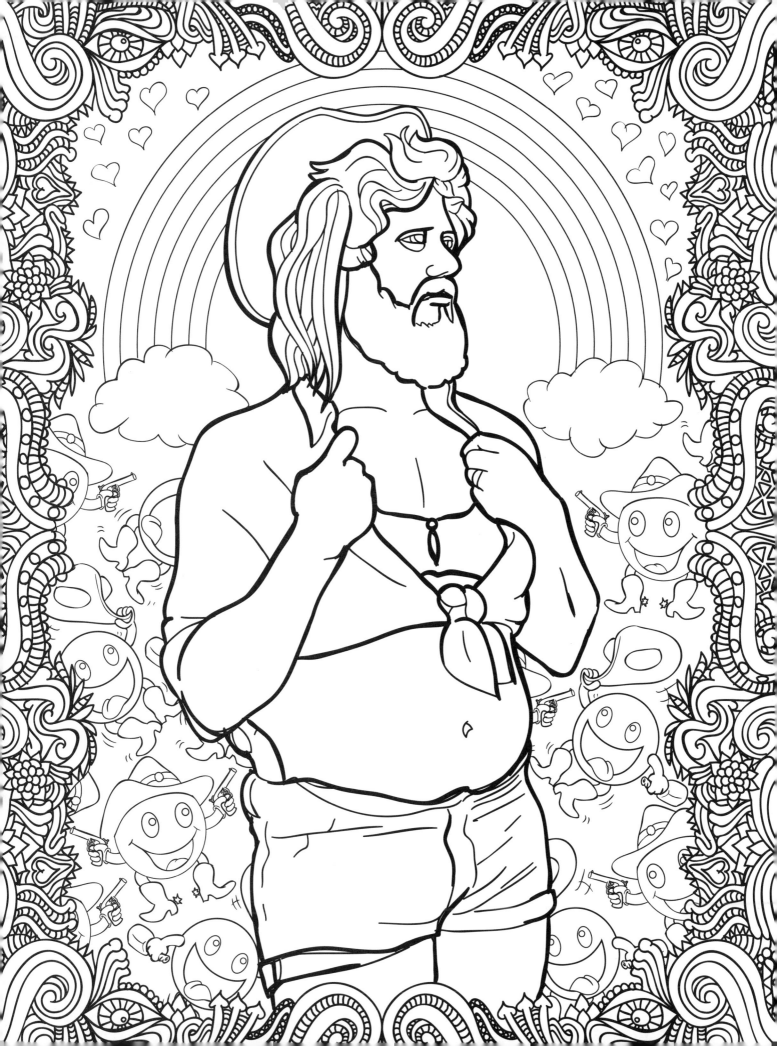

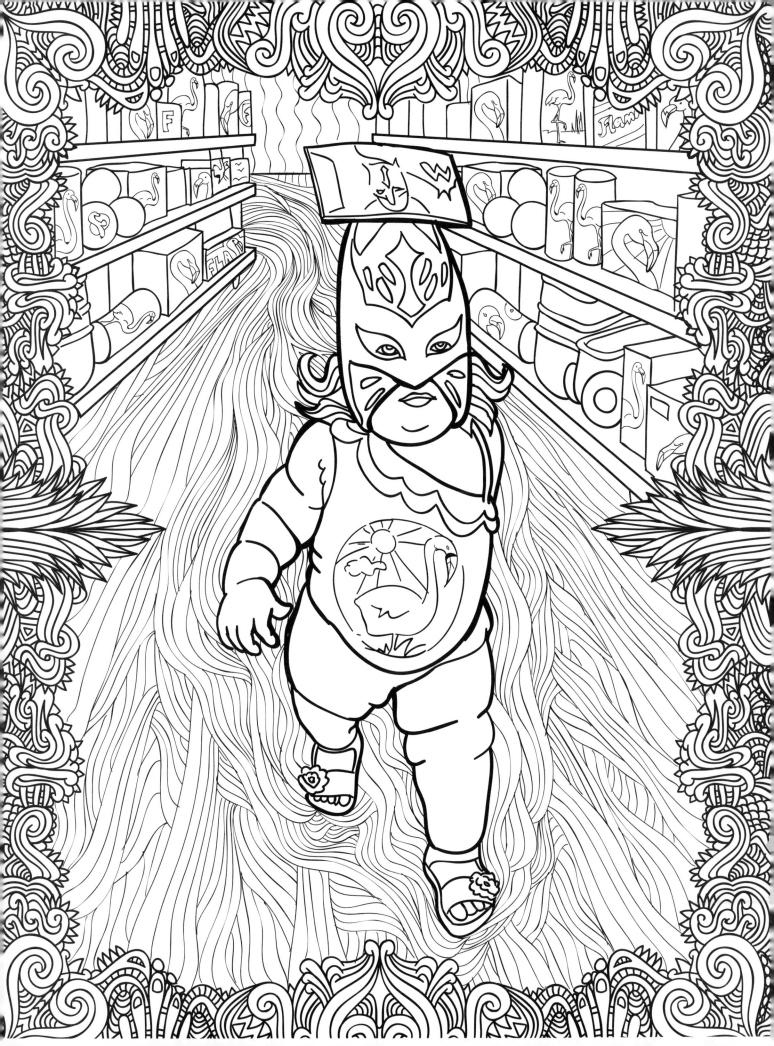

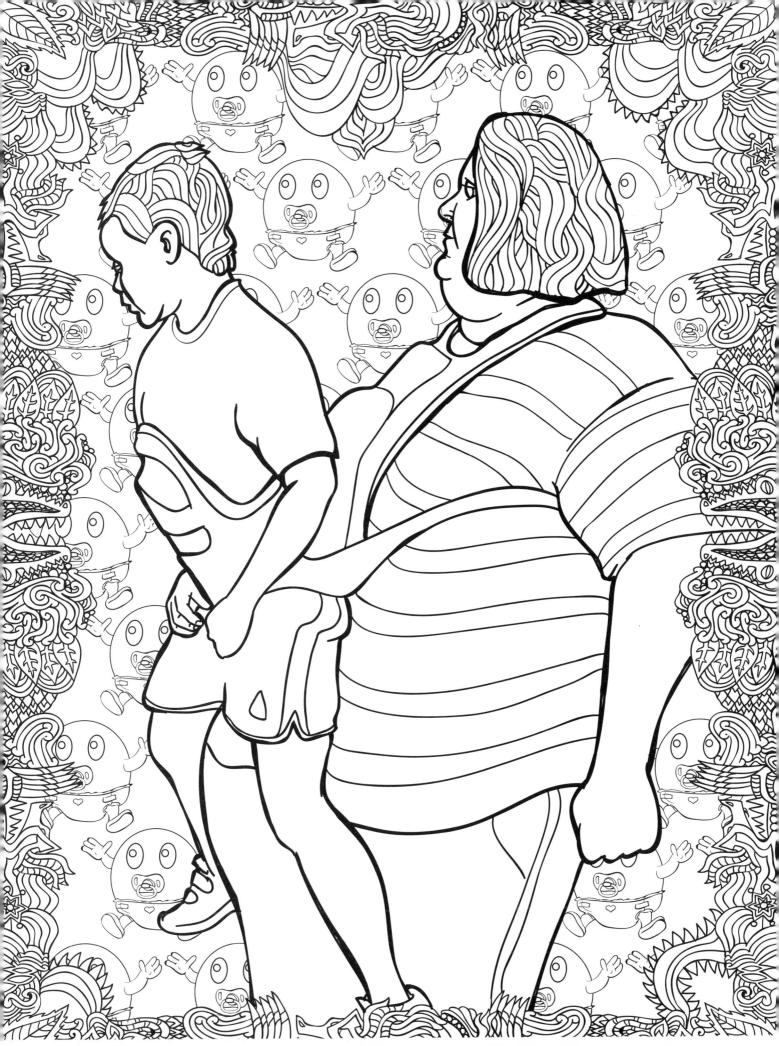

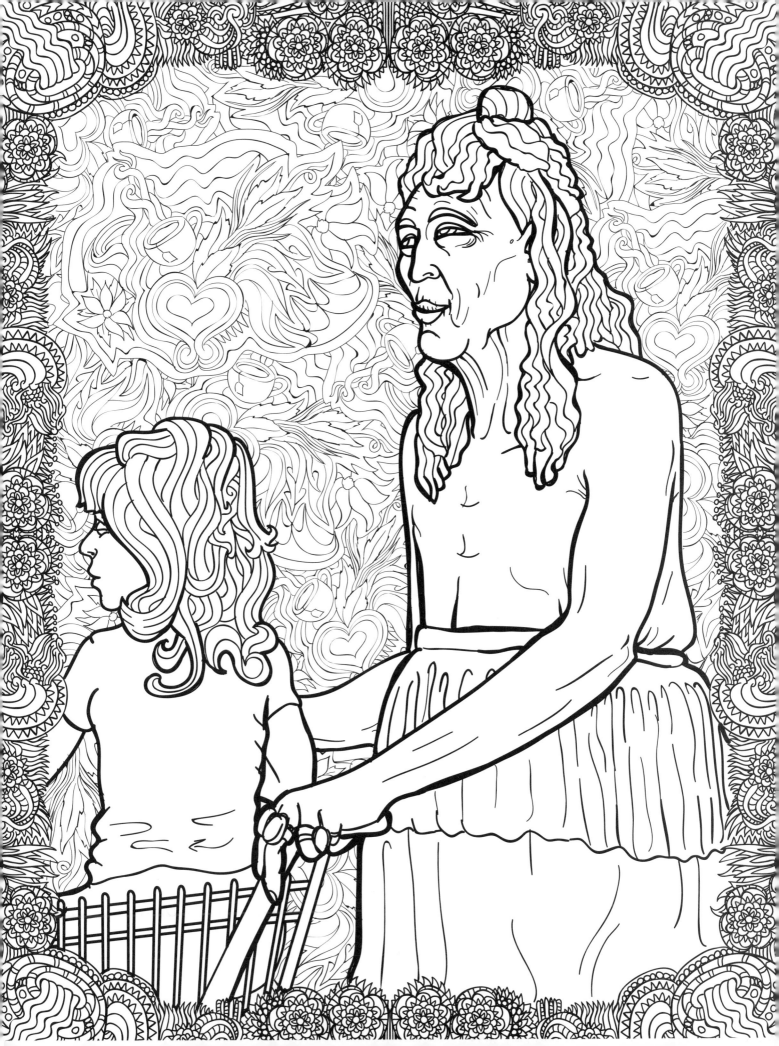

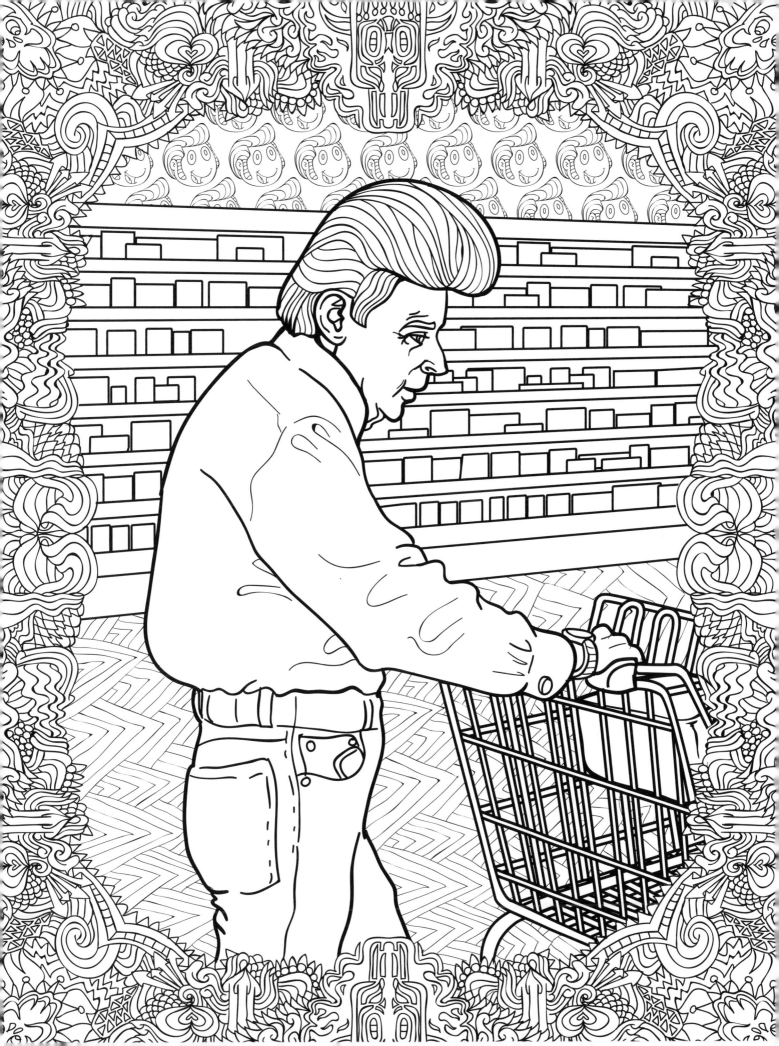

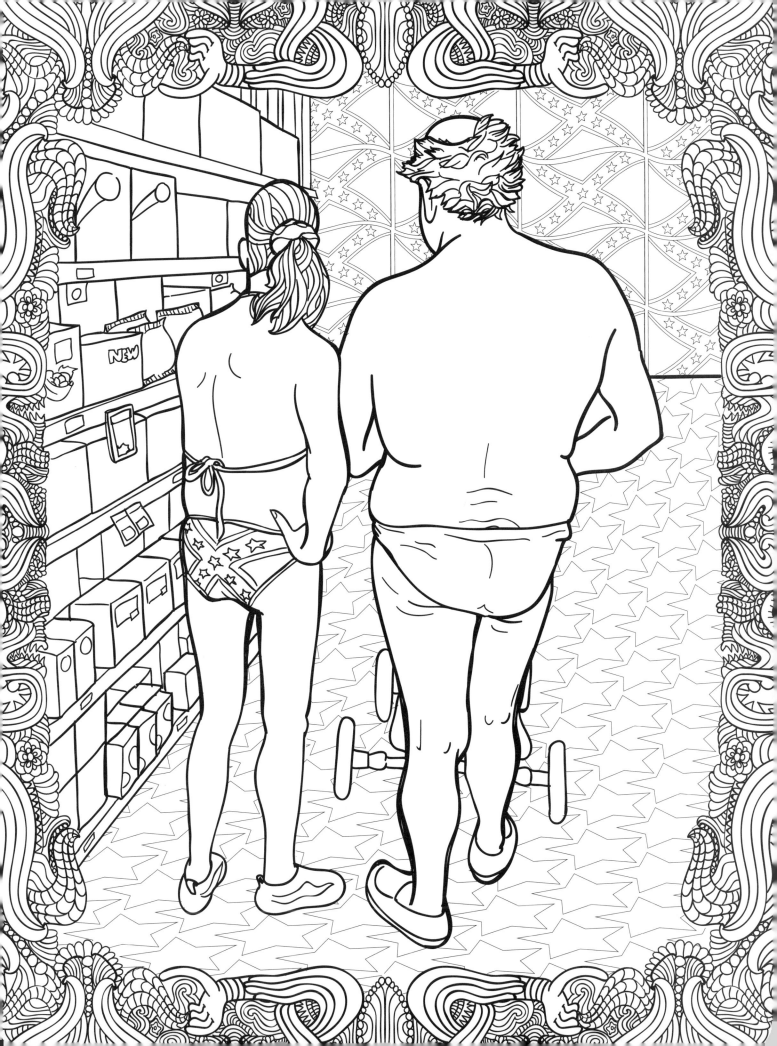

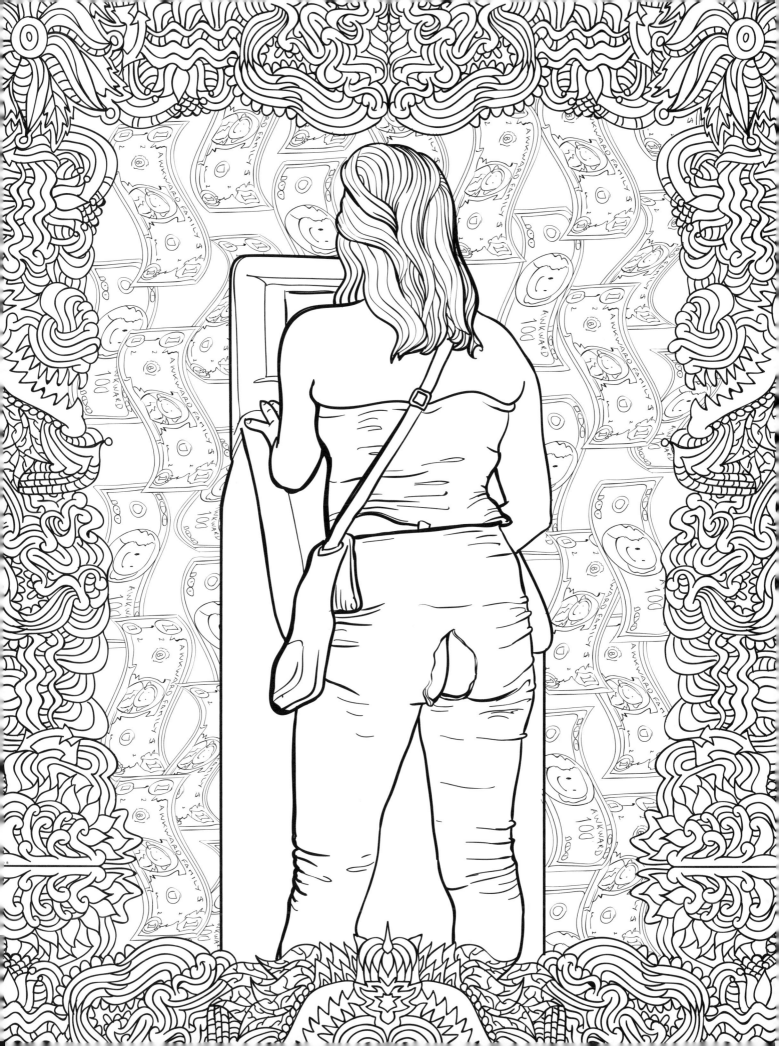

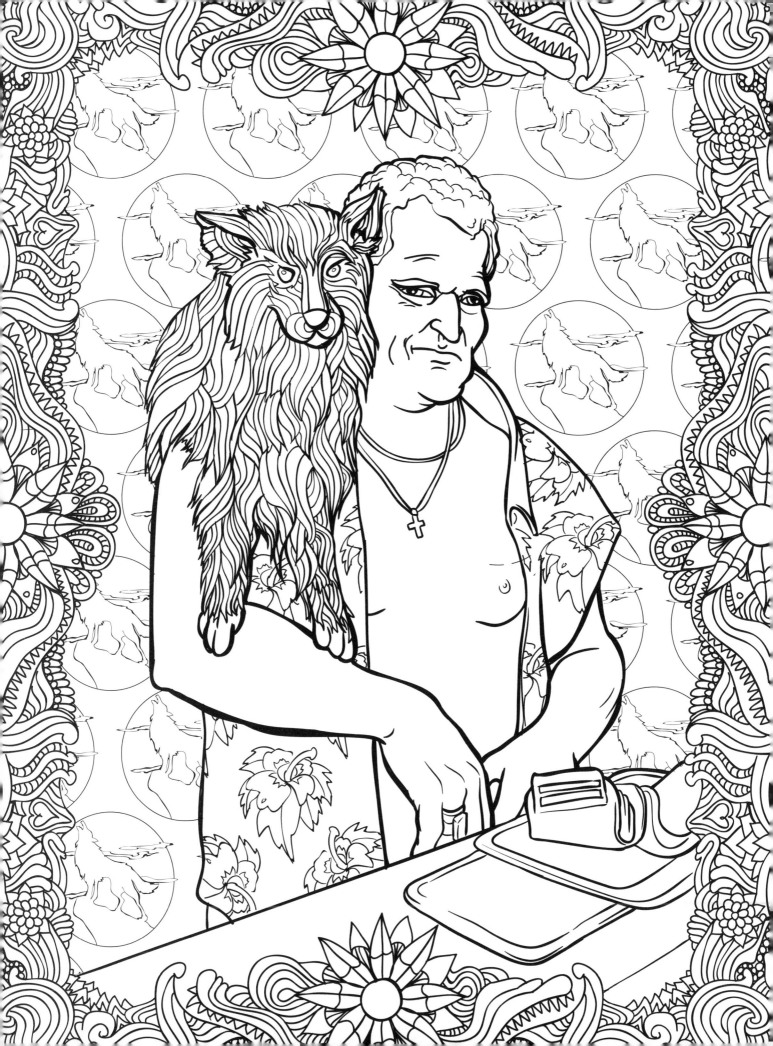

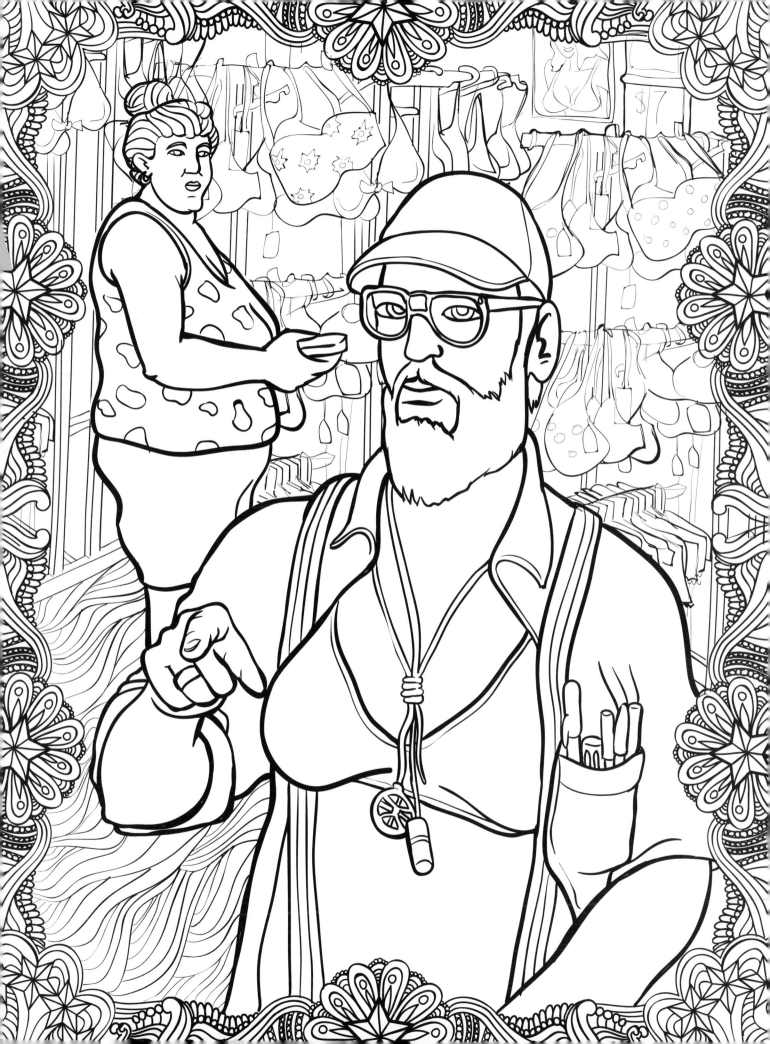

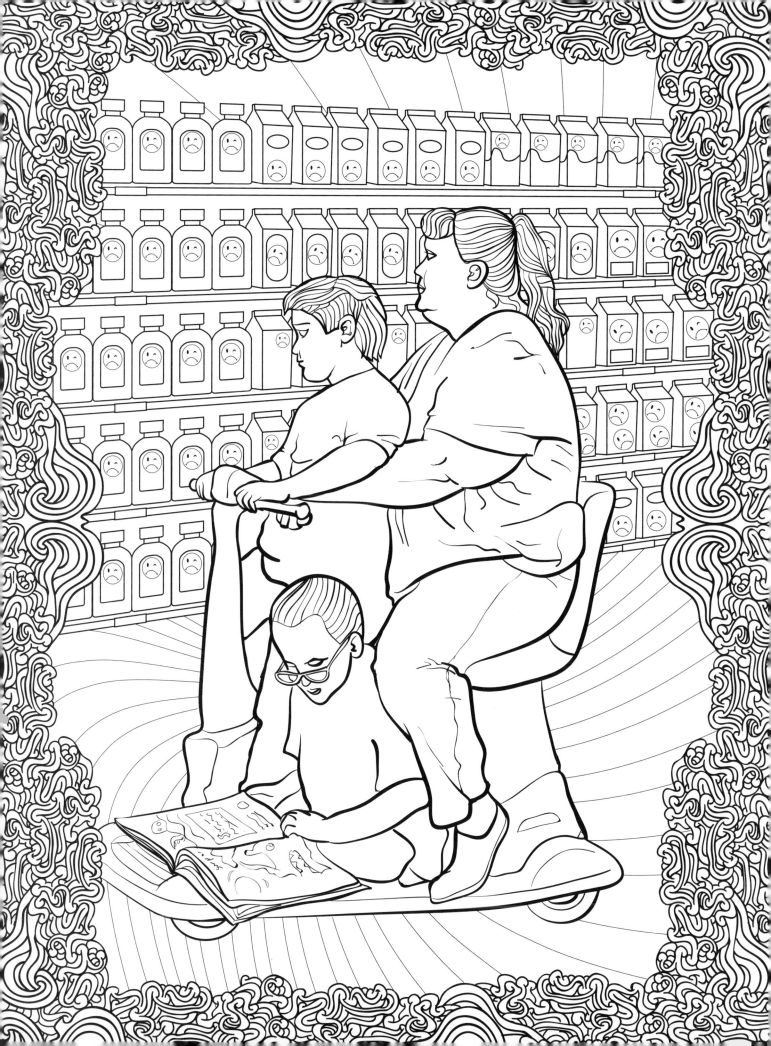

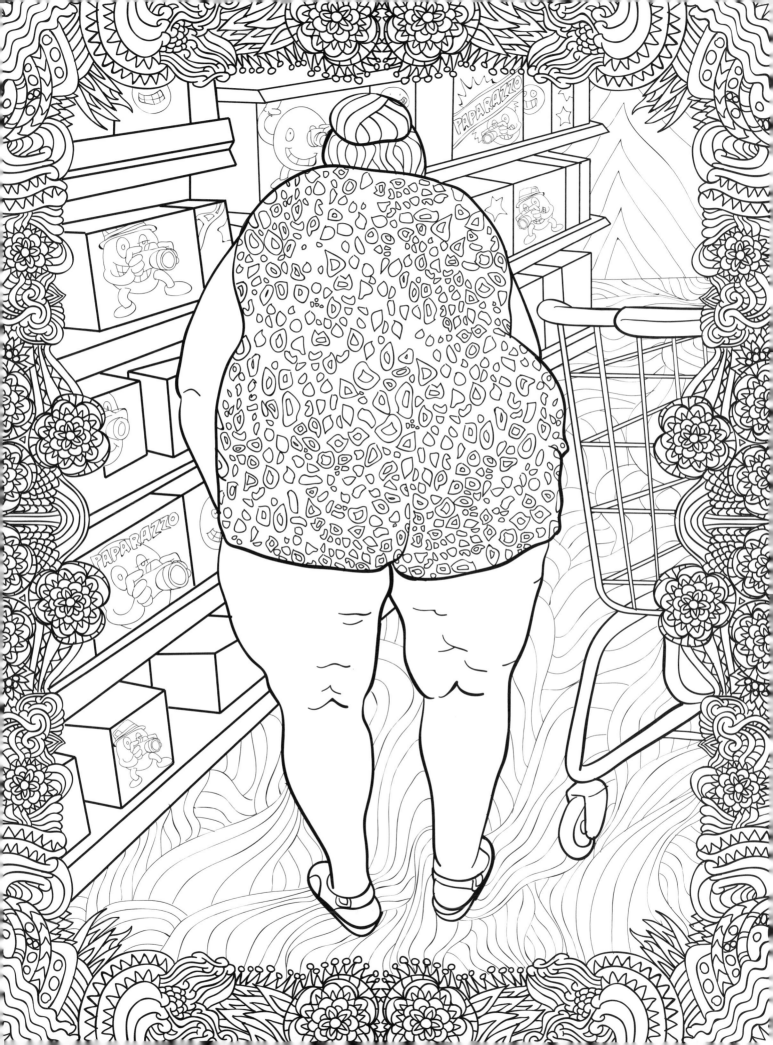

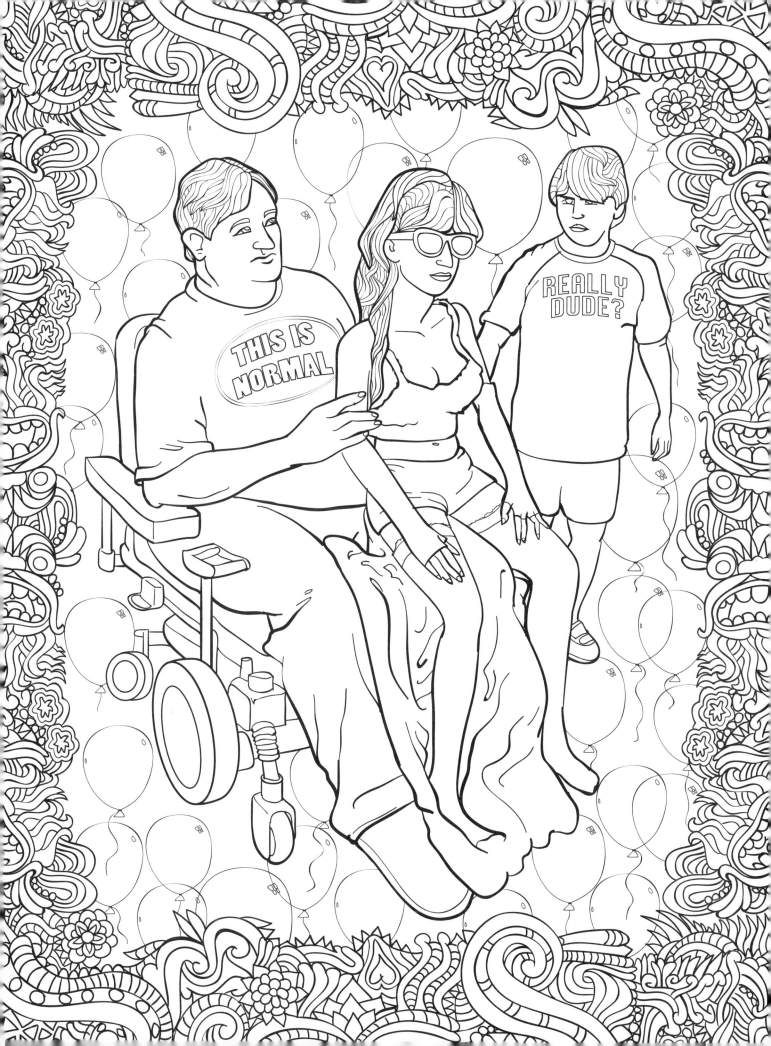

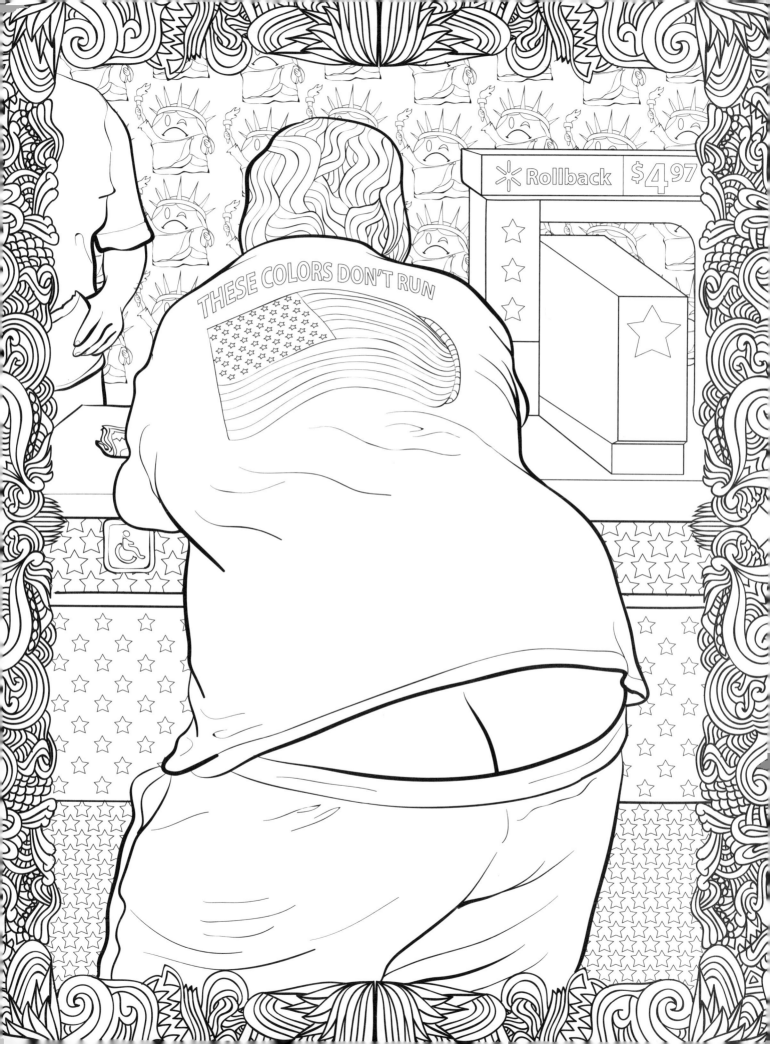

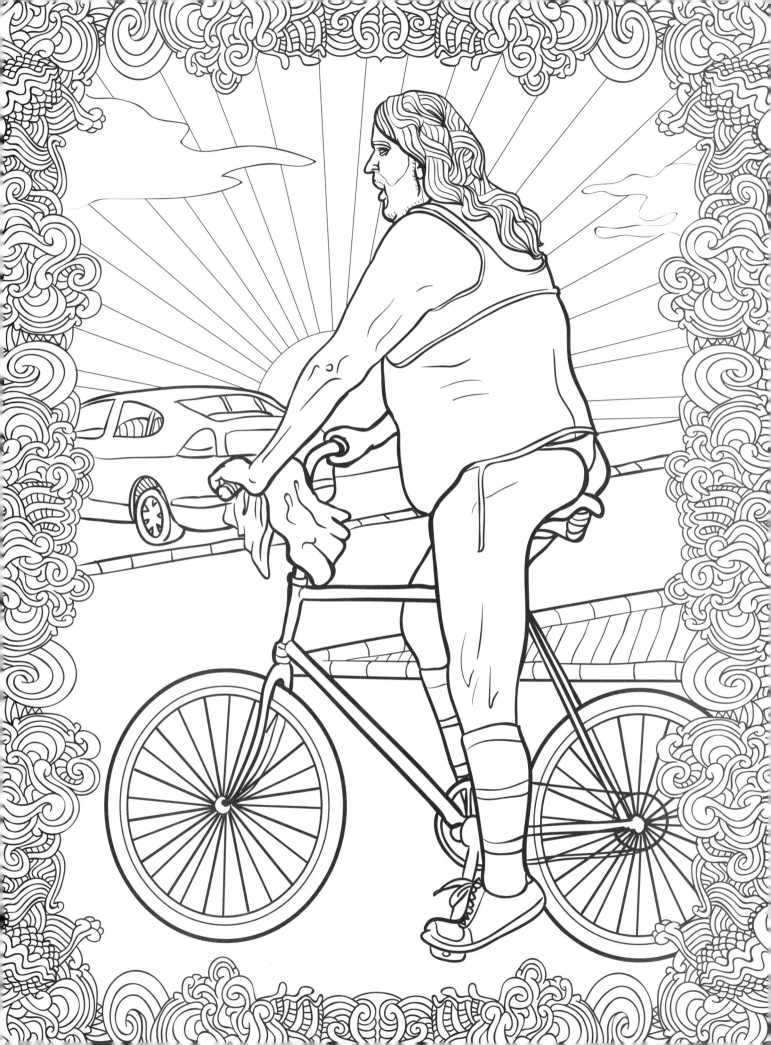

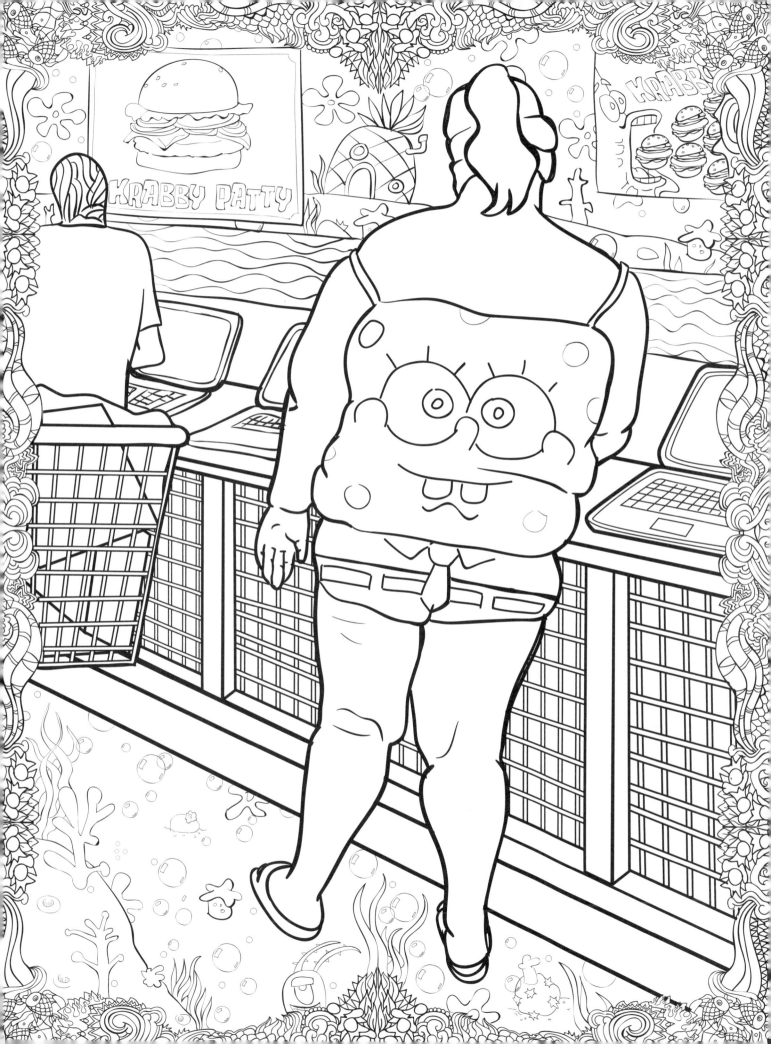

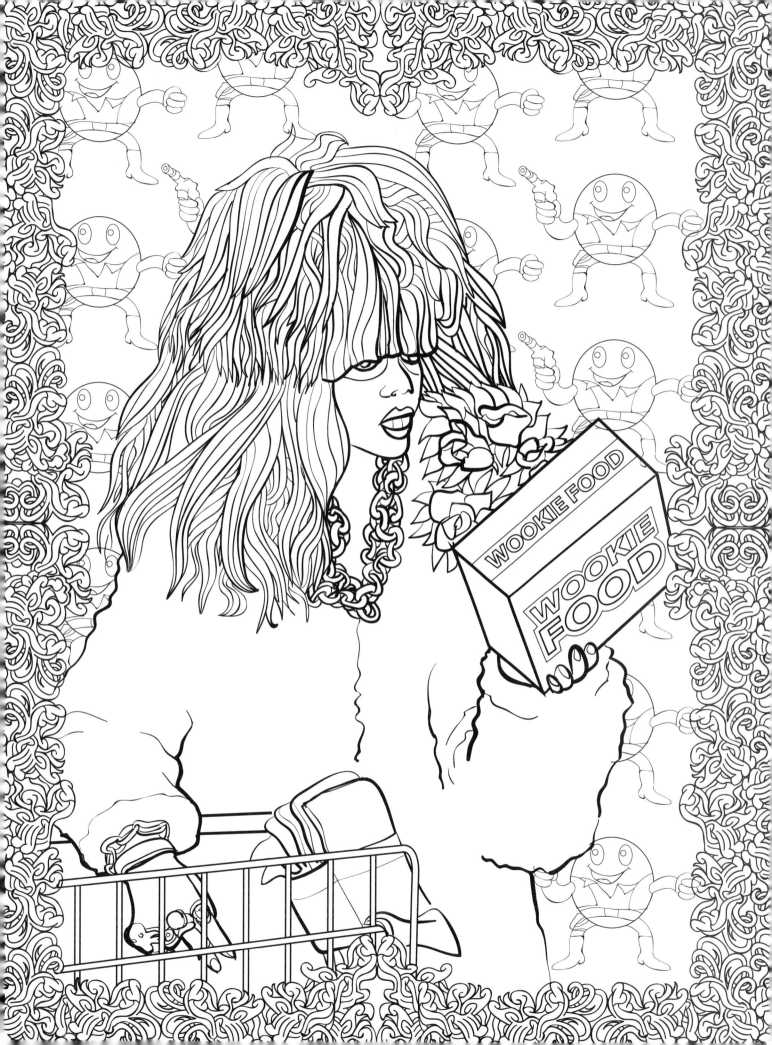

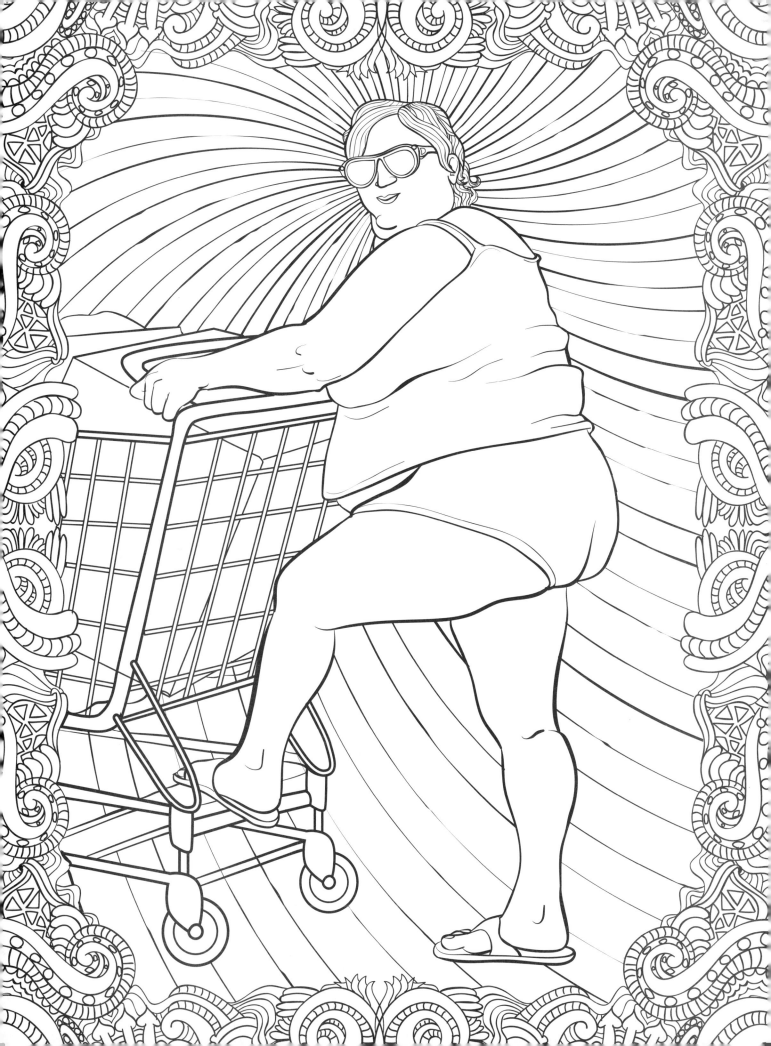

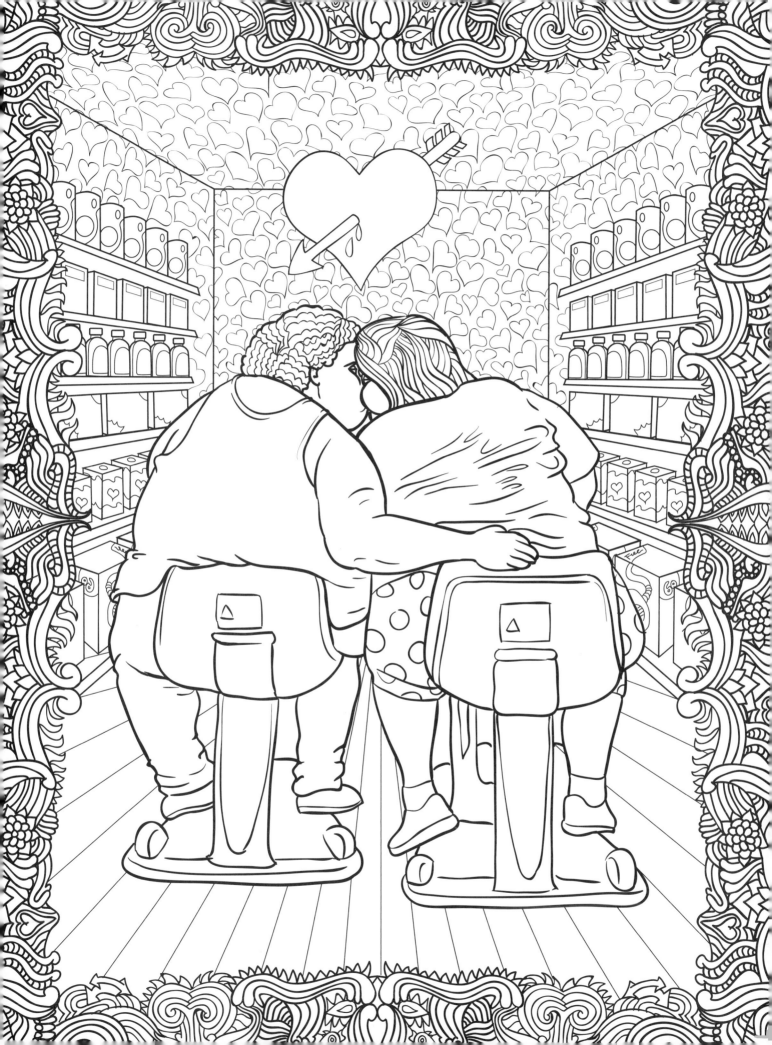

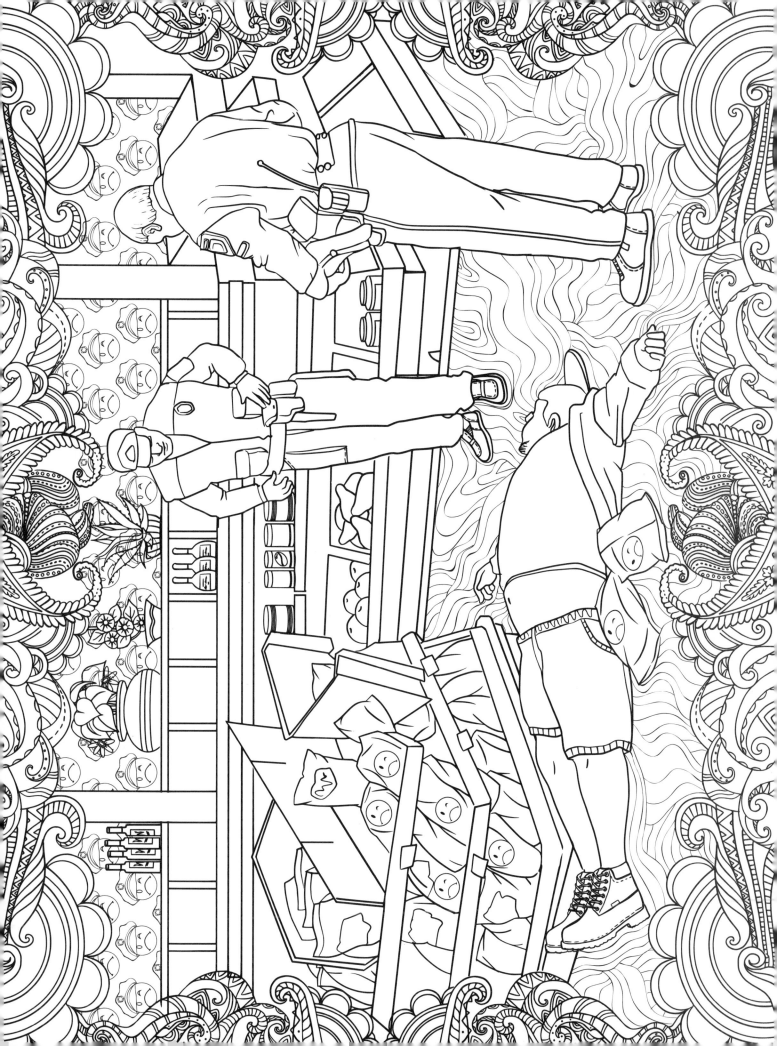

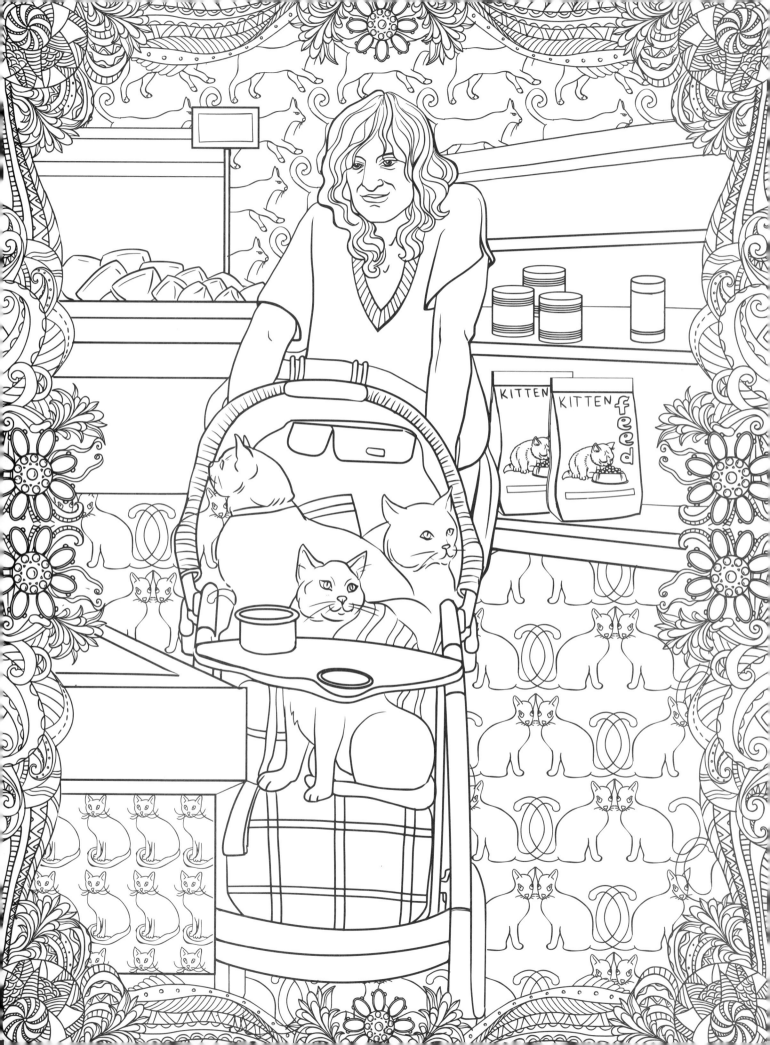

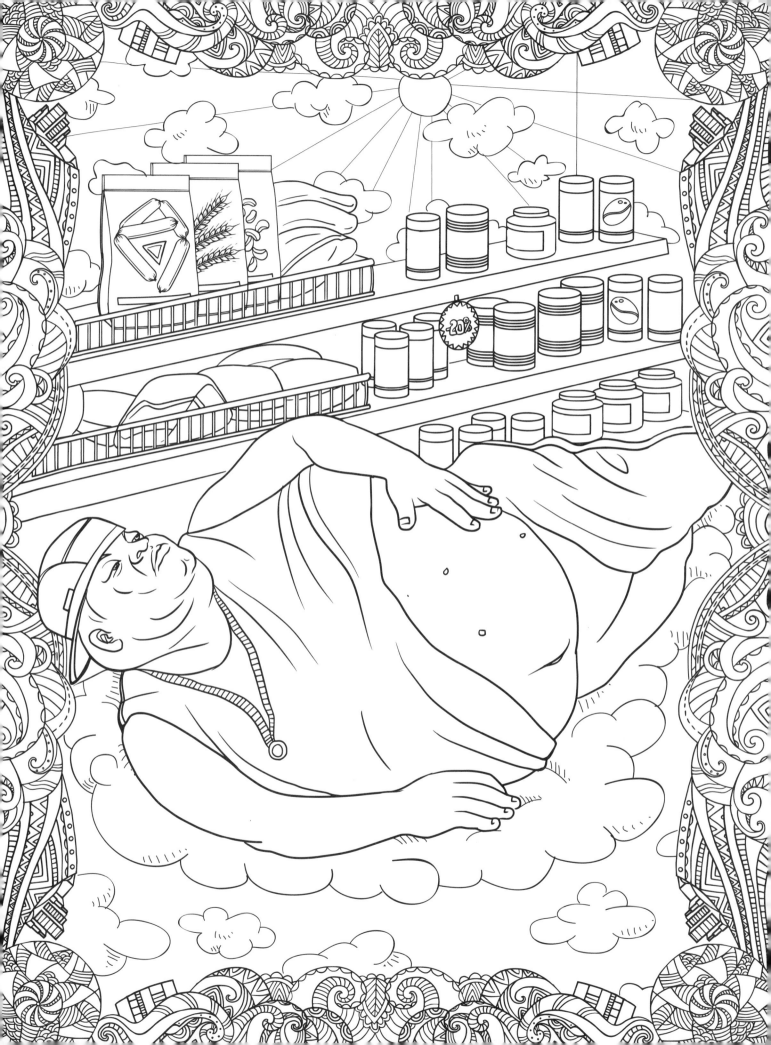

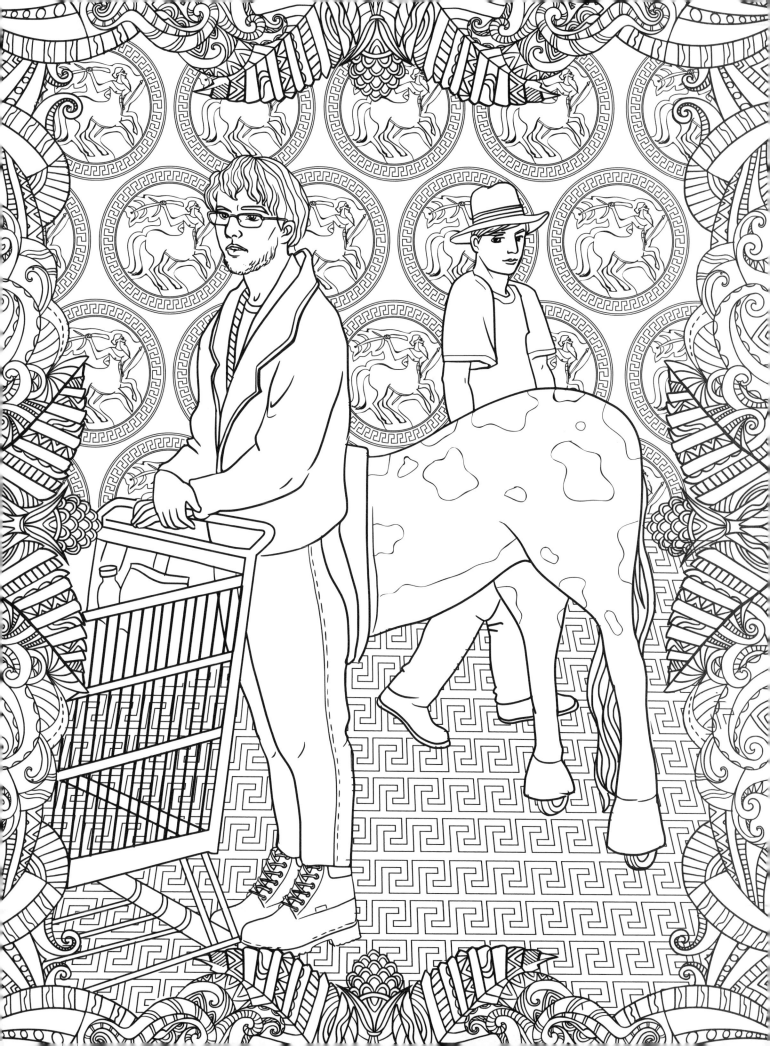

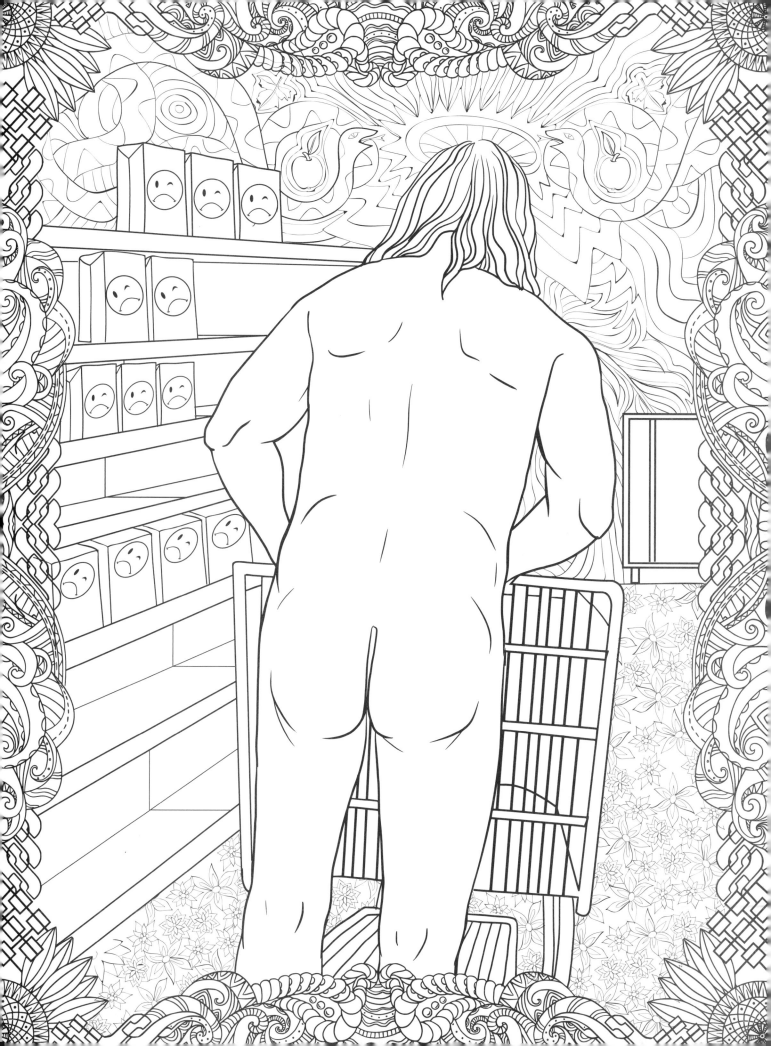

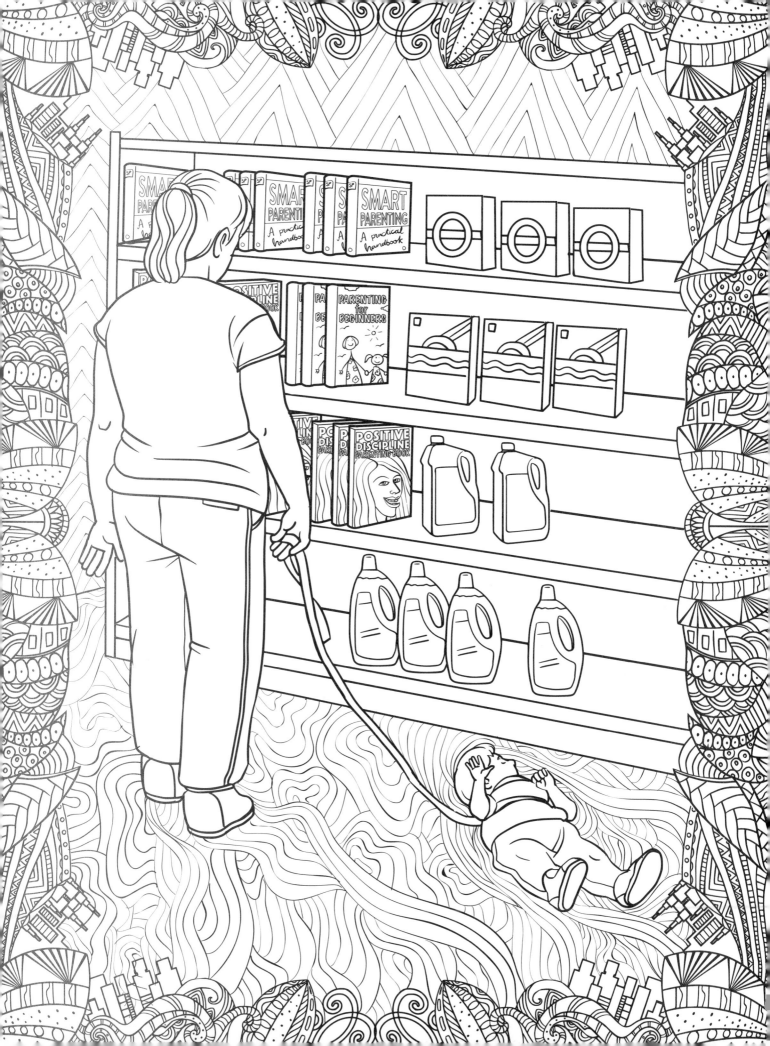

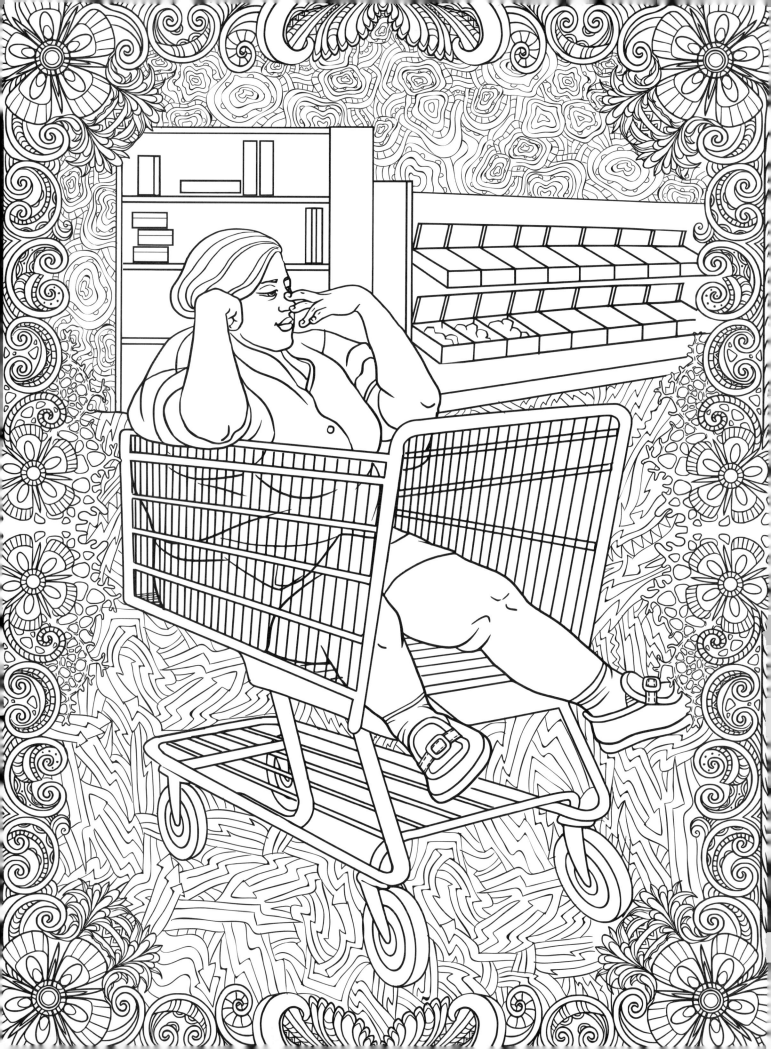

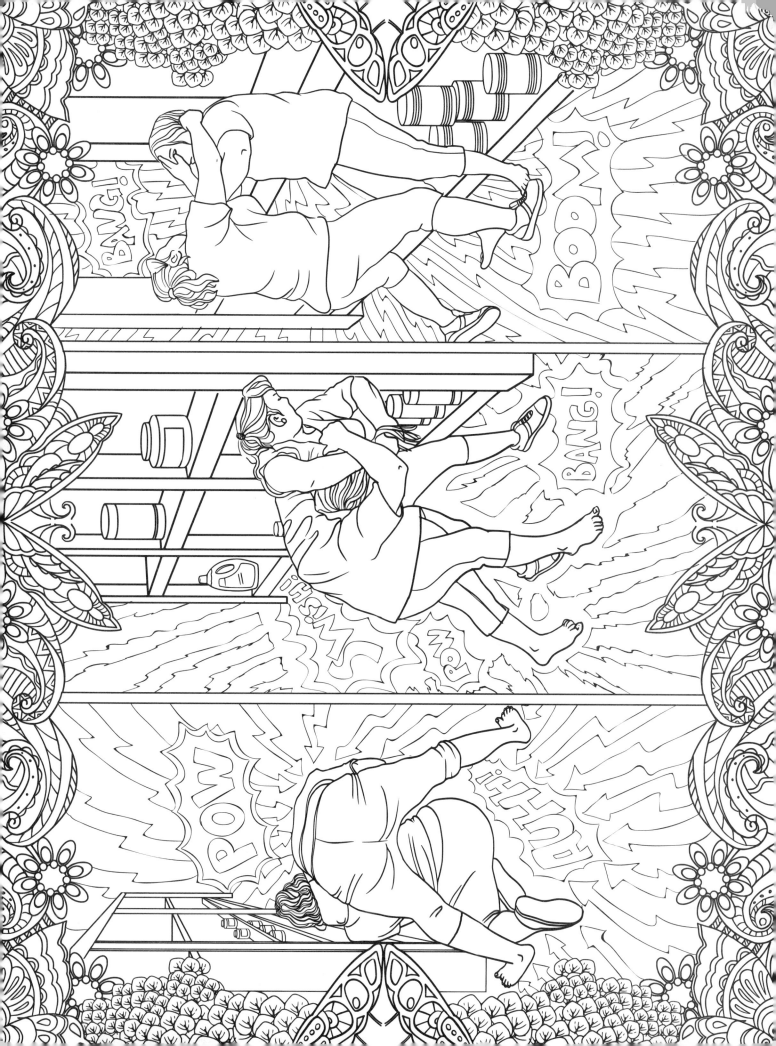

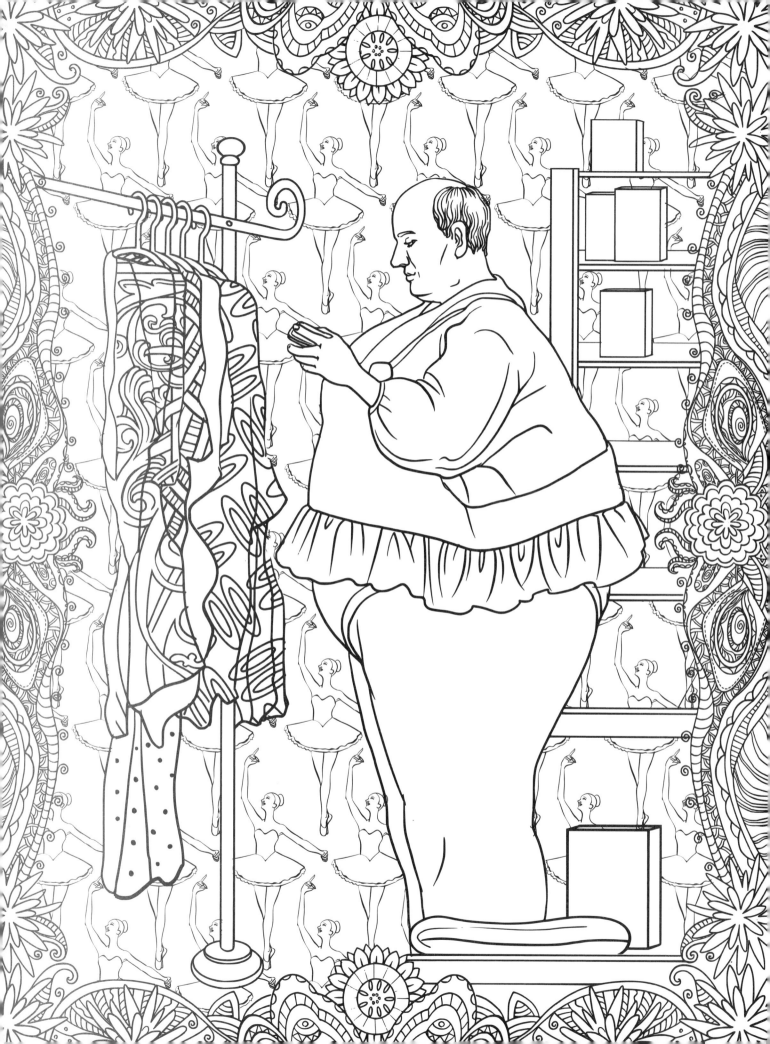

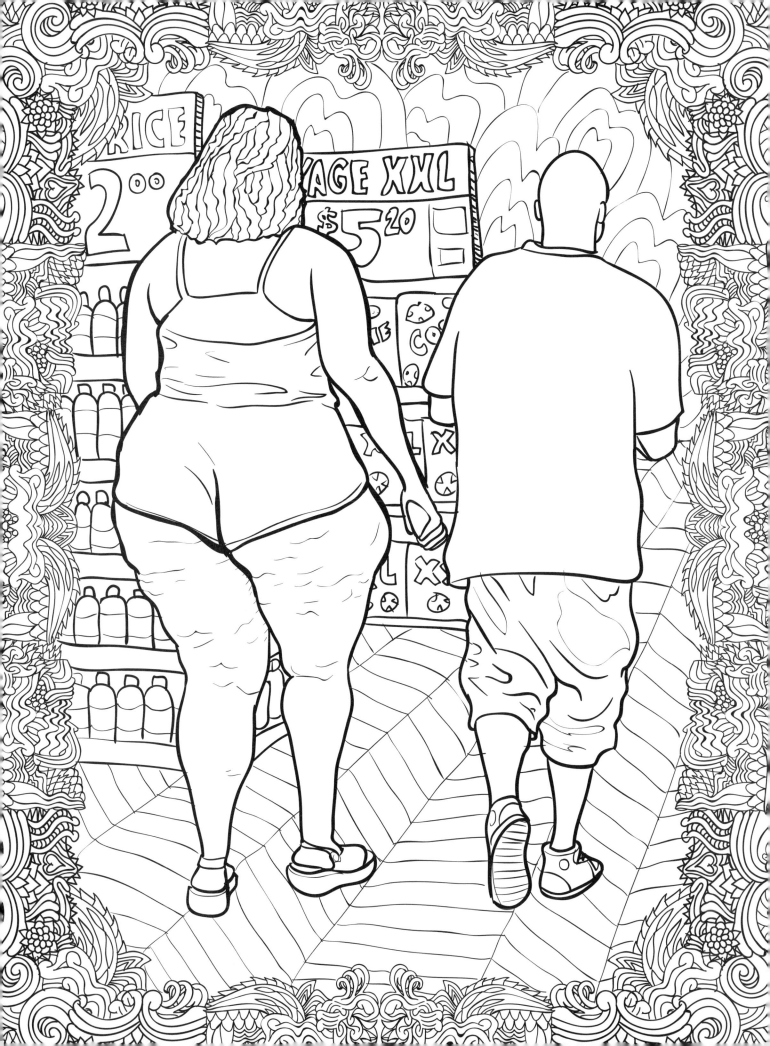

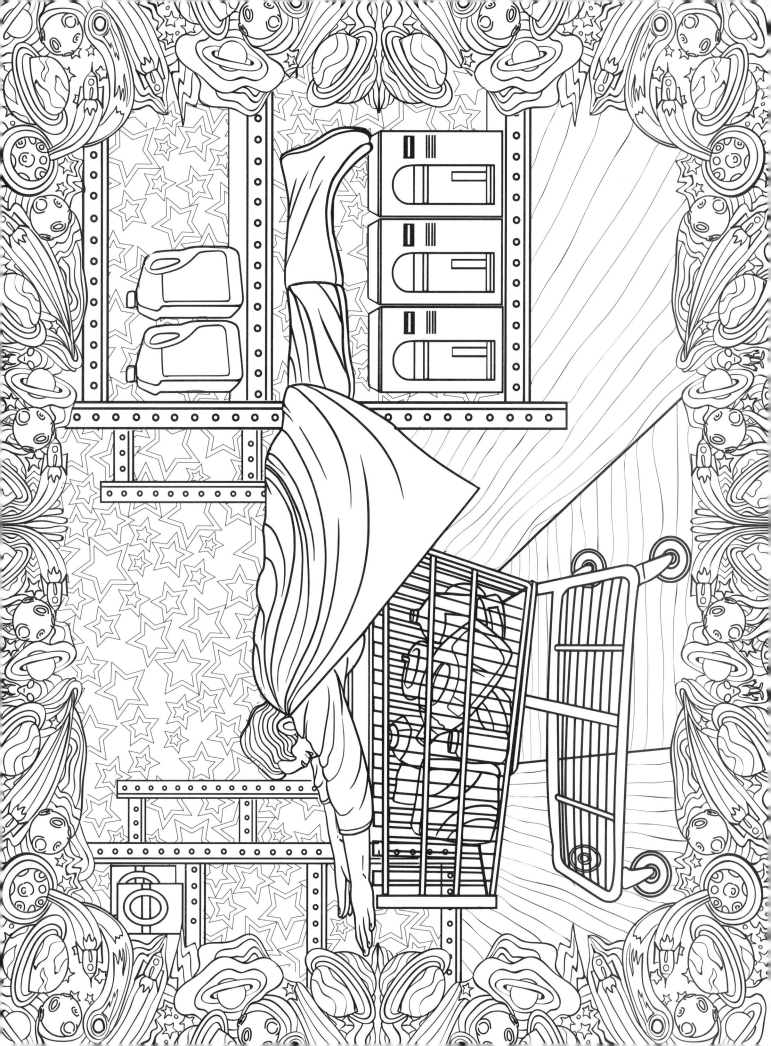

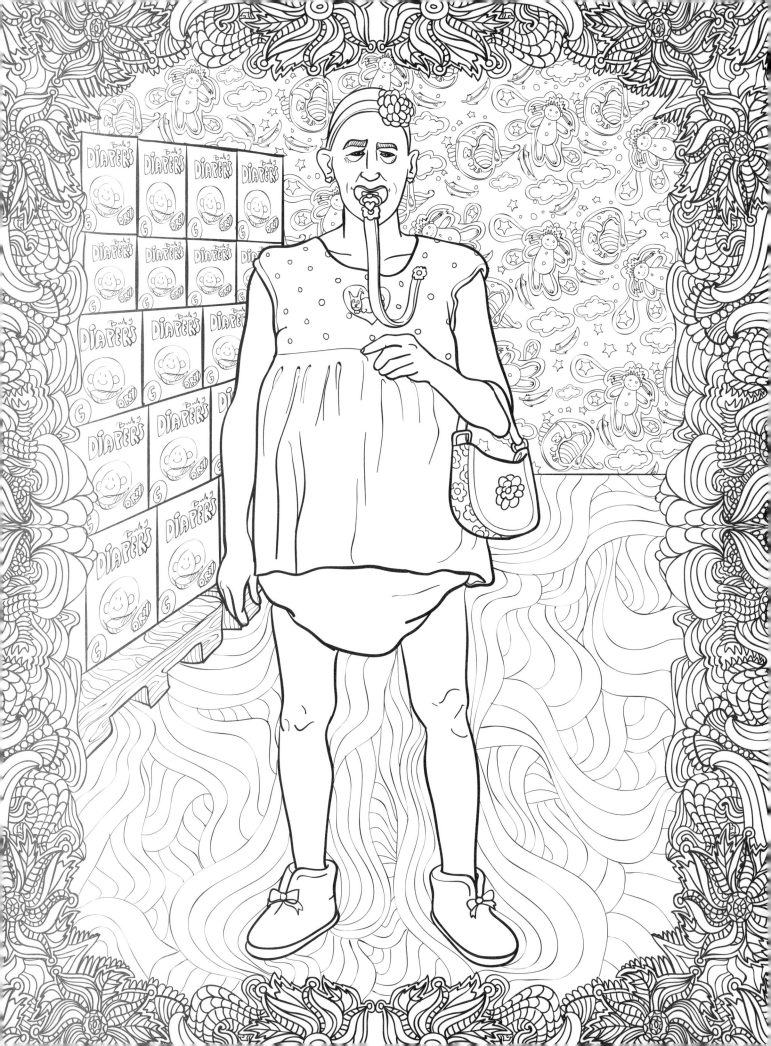

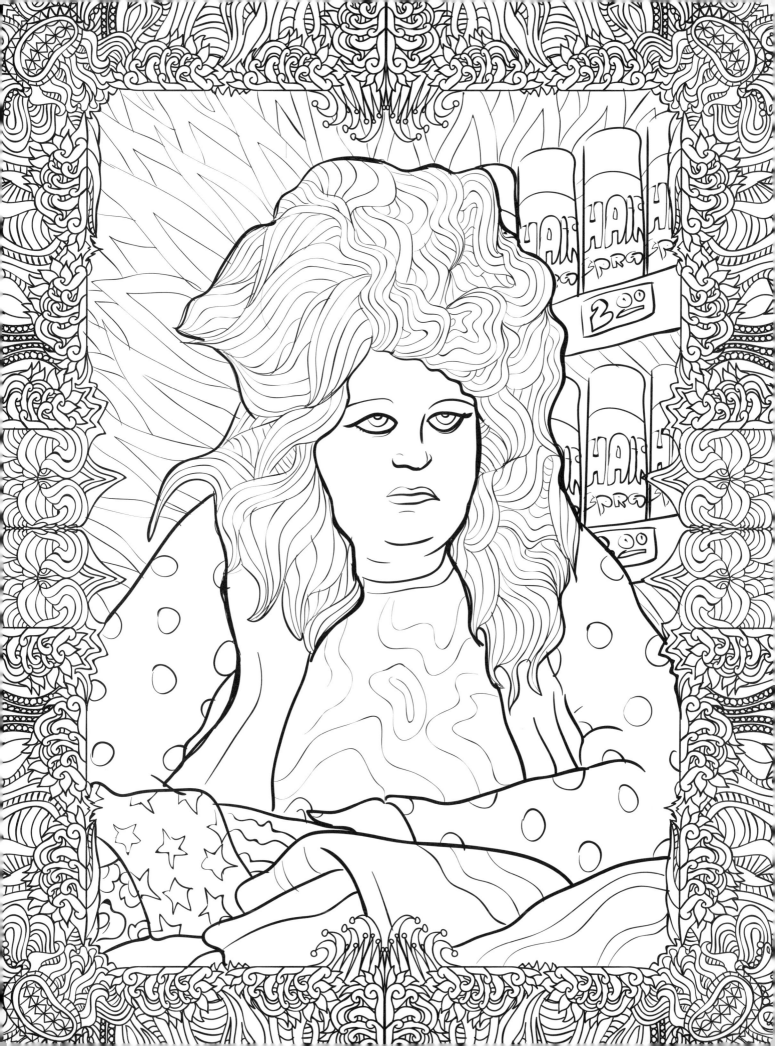

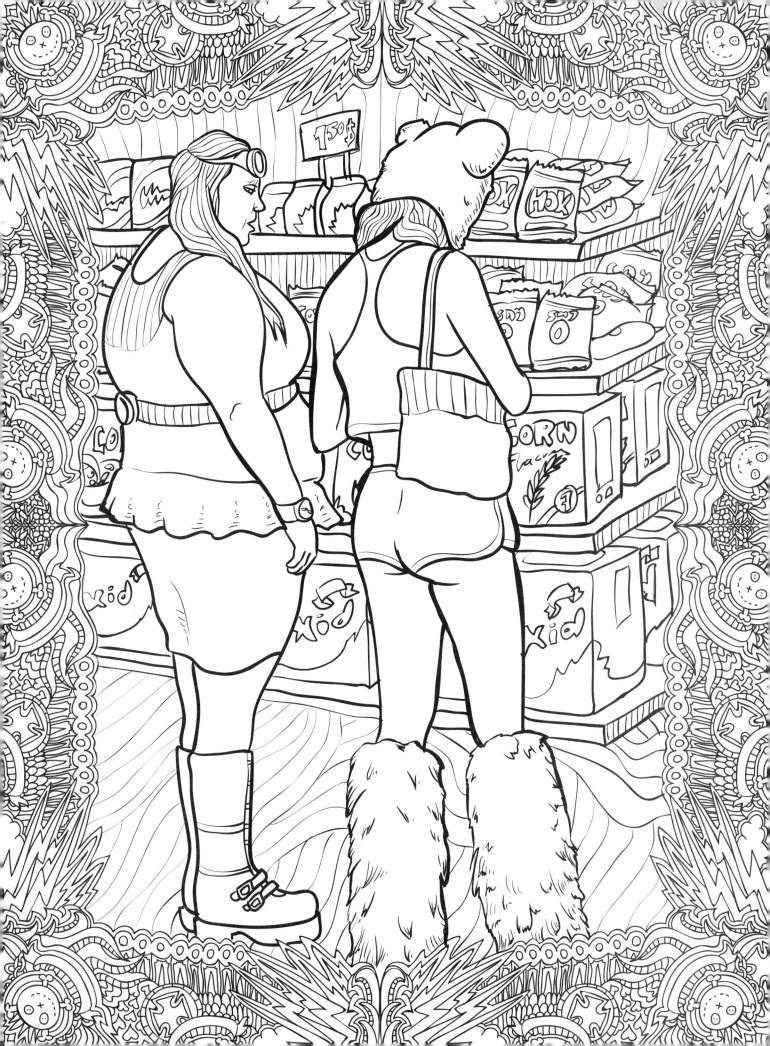

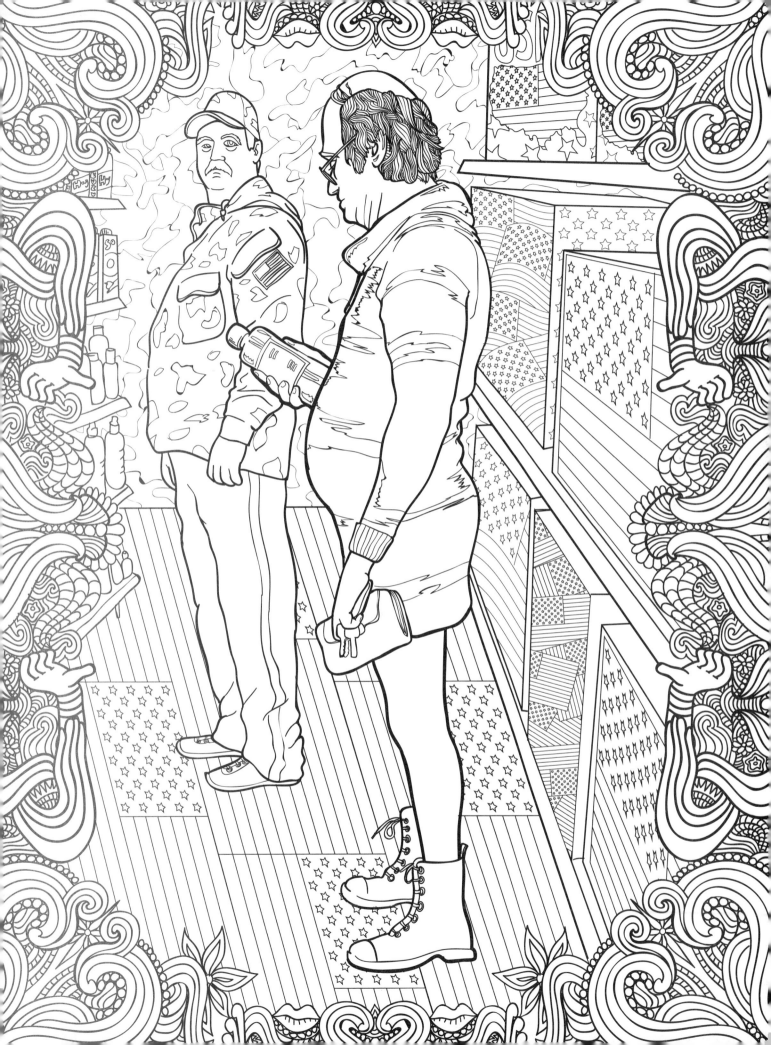

Check out these other hilarious adult coloring books from Day Drankin' Press also available on Amazon!

Hater Cats: An Insult Kitten Adult Coloring Book: A Healthy Way to Unleash Stress

Celebrity Mugshots: Keeping Up With The Incarcerated, An Adult Coloring Book

We think they're pretty good stuff.
But we're also a bit weird.

Well…not TOO weird,
I mean, we're not Marilyn Manson at a
4-year old's birthday party weird.

Maybe more like your friends who are weird cuz they know you and like you anyway.

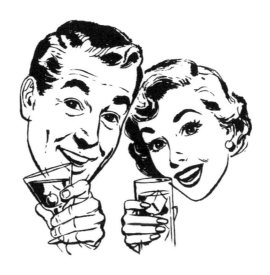